EMOTIONAL PARENTS OF ADULT KIDS: Ultimate guide on how to deal with Parents that are very Emotional.

Williams Bersus

Table of contents

1235

Chapter 1

The truth about emotional parents

Attachment" is a term used to describe the emotion that keeps us connected to the important people in our lives. The word "attach" can refer to tying, fastening, or connecting something to another in common usage. We may expect that the connecting rope, or the "connection," is robust enough to handle the task if one car were being towed by another. With a rope, every new thread that is woven in with the rest increases the rope's overall strength. Hundreds of tiny threads can be weaved together to form a practically unbreakable rope, despite their insignificance. The attachment bond between a parent and kid resembles a rope in many ways. The emotional bond between parent and child grows stronger with each successful encounter between them. They learn how to interpret varied encounters. They gain social skills that help them maintain current connections and build new ones. And they learn to be both self-reliant and to cooperate effectively with others. In summary, they build a range of talents that are not readily gained by direct teaching. Social and emotional skills are best learned via interactions.

Infancy is the optimal period to build a healthy bond. Not just because there is a lifetime ahead in the opportunity to make a difference, but also because of the enormous dependency of a newborn on adults. Because newborns rely on others to satisfy their needs, there are numerous chances for adults to emotionally immerse themselves in the connection while they care for them. Changing diapers, feeding, bathing, changing diapers, rocking, calming, and changing diapers all enable newborns to build trust and a loving adult to create commitment. Even the charming glances, modest grins, and baby fat seem almost engineered to keep parents near and interested. One observer noted, "we serve those we love and we love those we serve." So it is through the very act of attentive care that attachment is created.

Children may build a healthy bond with others without interfering with the parent-child relationship. A good bond with a child care provider may increase the attachment between parent and kld. Just as the abilities we develop at work may assist us at home, so may the social-emotional competencies obtained with compassionate childcare providers enhance the parent-child connection at home.

Although attachment develops in early infancy, the ties with people closest to us remain crucial throughout our lives. One of the early studies of attachment, John Bowlby, observed humans, from cradle to the grave, are happiest when life is arranged as a series of excursions, long or short, from a stable foundation given by our attachment figure(s)."

Parents and loving individuals may do many things to develop a bond. Here are a few

Take care of yourself. It is tough to reach out and build a connection with our children if we're swamped with personal concerns. At times our concentration on personal difficulties may compel us to turn inward. Parents who are sad, lonely, or have marital troubles are more likely to have difficulty building good bonds. However, taking care of ourselves doesn't necessarily imply concentrating on ourselves. Sometimes the greatest treatment for ourselves is being with and assisting others-especially our children.
Follow your child's lead. Every partnership is a dance. When one moves, the other moves in synchrony. The finest dancers learn to detect and react to tiny signals. The same applies to relationships. When a youngster grins with joy, smile back with the same passion. When your kid communicates sentiments of hurt, react to the emotional distress with compassion and care. As you react carefully to your kid's behavior, your youngster will also learn to behave correctly to others.
Be responsive to your child's needs. Attachment parenting is attentive to a child's needs. In infancy, infants typically convey their needs by crying. They may cry because they are hungry, exhausted, need a diaper change, or just need to be soothed. It is impossible to be

overly attentive to children in infancy. As children get older, separating needs from desires may be increasingly complicated. Understanding child growth in general, and your kid's development in particular, can help you be sensitive without spoiling (see the section on spoiling in this series) (see the unit on spoiling in this series).Animate life. Young children typically have a tough time identifying the slight difference between distinct emotional expressions. Using exaggerated facial expressions or nonverbal clues can help your youngster learn crucial lessons about communicating and understanding emotions. Understanding and reacting correctly to emotions is the cornerstone for sustaining relationships.

Spend time playing with your youngster. Nothing expresses love like the time spent with your kid. Make time to play together, read together, work together, learn together, and hug together. Simply spend plenty of time together. Planned quality time is vital, but it is frequently during lengthy car drives or other unexpected times that children open up and express their deepest wants and worries. The relevance of the amount of time should not be ignored. As one individual put it, "The secret to being a great parent is to be a decent person and then stay around your kids.

Chapter 2

Children start forming their emotions during the infancy period, which lasts about from birth to the age of two years. During this period, a tremendous lot of basic learning happens for the infant, about their overall surroundings and the individuals who are in them. Much of this learning comes via interactions with parents and observations of parental connections, who are the earliest and most important individuals in a child's early life. Happiness, sorrow, and disgust are amongst the early feelings to arise in youngsters within a few months after birth. Later on, social emotions arise followed by a sense of dread between the ages of two and four years. Generally, feelings start to vary as a youngster starts to age.

So far, it is known that parents considerably impact the emotional development of their children. Parents do considerably more than supply the fundamental survival requirements of their kids, and research is increasingly discovering that parents have a huge effect on a broad range of health outcomes for their children, including behavioral patterns, physical and mental health outcomes, and emotional development. In the last few decades, enormous effort and study have gone into understanding how inter-parental conflict could impair a children's capacity to grow, develop and operate healthily. For instance, over two-thirds of all research included in one author's meta-analysis that linked to the inter-parental conflict was published in the 1990s, illustrating just how much interest has developed in recent years for this topic.

In this respect, it is vital to bridge the gap in information about what sorts of parental actions impact the emotional development of their children, and in what ways. It is crucial to examine how good and bad parenting behavior impacts the emotional development of children. As Fincham (2001) writes, "This is a particularly appropriate moment to review the present situation of the discipline and to anticipate future directions". In this specific study, it will be studied whether and how inter-parental disagreements affect the emotional stability and development of their children.

This study article will undertake a meta-analysis of current literature to address the essential question: can inter-parental conflict adversely influence the emotional stability of children who are members of the family?

Children's exposure to inter-parental conflict seems to be high internationally and growing. For instance, in Australia, experts have discovered that inter-parental conflict impacts millions of children yearly. The frequency of reported domestic violence cases in Australia has grown in the previous six years. Statistics reveal that approximately a percent of women endure violence that is perpetrated by a spouse at some time in their life, and that this impacts a minimum of one million children annually. These estimates certainly indicate a major understatement, considering that family conflict statistics are derived from the police, child welfare, and family court data, which only covers the most severe kinds of psychological, physical, and emotional abuse. Researchers like Westrupp have determined that the frequency of inter-parental conflict is likely far greater than these figures show.

Increasingly there has also been a significantly greater worldwide acknowledgment of the tremendous health costs and economic repercussions that both high and low-lying levels of inter-parental conflict may produce. For instance, women who are often exposed to violence within their family are recognized as being at a greater risk of suffering major and long-term unfavorable mental and physical health consequences. Research also reveals that allegations of domestic violence are likely to arise for parents who are younger, less educated, originate from single or divorced homes, and have greater levels of stress and alcohol-related disorders. For children, the health effects associated with inter-parental conflict are numerous and include (but are not limited to) increased prevalence of mental health problems such as mood and anxiety disorders, attention deficit hyperactivity disorder, conduct or oppositional defiant disorder, as well as several physical health problems such as obesity, asthma, and accidental injury.

While much of the previous literature has concentrated on the most severe examples of domestic abuse-which could involve physical, emotional, and sexual abuse-researchers are increasingly correlating lower levels of inter-parental conflict to challenging child development. Thus, psychologists are increasingly realizing that inter-parental conflict may encompass less severe but much more prevalent kinds of conflict, including verbal conflict (such as disputes, rage, hostility, or fights) and lower degrees of physical violence (such as pushing, kicking, slapping or shoving) (such as pushing, kicking, hitting or shoving). As such, studies on this subject are progressively becoming more generalizable to the rest of the population.

Researchers and doctors have long thought that there is an essential association between the quality of parental interactions and the emotional, physical, cognitive, and psychological development of their children. The association between inter-parental conflict and children's behavioral and emotional development disorders has been well-established for both intact and divorced homes]. Meta-analysis had shown that the average impact size for inter-parental conflict on child development was between a small and medium effect which is approximately twice the effect size for the link between child adjustment and divorce. The inter-parental conflict has been reported to be higher for homes with children who are under the age of five years. Inter-parental and parent-child conflicts have been found to negatively impact children across all ages in terms of emotional, social, academic, and health problems, and children's risk becomes particularly high when parents are involved in a highly distressed marriage.

Try our contributing to the unfavorable development outcomes of children. As such, a more recent study has aimed to uncover the features of children who are exposed to inter-parental conflict, as well as their coping mechanisms and contextual elements of the inter-parental conflict that may be impacting their adjustment issues. Findings imply that rather than being the conflict itself that is leading to issues, there are more proximal mechanisms that account for the association between inter-parental conflict and the appearance of child behavioral disorders.

Researchers like Rhoades have discovered that when examining the consequences of inter-parental conflict on children's emotional development, it is more effective to examine children's reactions to conflict as one possible proximal variable. These reactions demonstrate how children are digesting and constructing meaning from the inter-parental conflict they encounter, especially regarding their own goals, wishes, and needs. According to Rhoades, children's reactions to conflict are crucial because:Children's responses to [inter-parental conflict] are most proximal to their own psychosocial and physical adjustments,\s These responses provide an index of how children interpret and cope with [inter-parental conflict], which should

ultimately mediate the relation between [inter-parental conflict] and child adjustment, and
The literature on adult connections to [inter-parental conflict] is sufficiently substantial to support a thorough, quantitative evaluation and offers an established theoretical basis.

Research has increasingly focused on how parents express and handle disagreement in their relationship. Although conflict is present in nearly every relationship, it frequently gets more severe and frequent when relationship quality begins to diminish. An adult who watches inter-parental conflict has claimed that it is a big stressor, and several studies have shown that children will express stress when they are exposed to violent or furious interactions that include their parents. The inter-parental conflict has been demonstrated to be a greater predictor of children's development difficulties than a marital breakup, suggesting that ongoing exposure to the conflict may be more unpleasant for a kid than going through a divorce in the family].

Emotional development in children is something that is to a large part acquired since children through time learn to manage their emotions. Most of this learning happens immediately through witnessing and interacting with parents, who are the first and most important persons in a child's early life. According to Moges & Weber, "children witness how their parents show emotions and interact with other people, and they emulate what they see their parents do to manage emotions". While a child's temperament might impact their capacity to manage their emotions, it is primarily led by the parenting methods that they get and the interactions they watch. Children who are more prone to negative emotions might be especially exposed to moments of rage or aggressive and inattentive parenting and relationships, making the significance of emotional and behavioral control even more obvious in such circumstances

Rhoades has discovered that hostile subjective perceptions of inter-parental conflict may be highly connected with children's behavioral and emotional issues. These findings led them to develop the Emotional Security Hypothesis (EST), which assumes that "children's reactions to [inter-parental conflict] are a function of the perceived implications of the conflict on the well-being of the family and have the goal of preserving and promoting the child's emotional security". The cognitions that a youngster develops to identify with their endangered feeling of home stability over time will trigger a dread and helplessness response that may later become generalized to a larger range of life circumstances. Adults may also acquire cognitions of danger and self-blame that may become related to internalized behavioral difficulties. If children begin to believe that they are responsible for their parents' problems, they may frequently experience guilt, shame, and grief that severely affect their emotional well-being and development.

While little is known about how inter-parental conflict might impact the physical health outcomes of children, investigations have revealed that these two elements are regularly associated. This might occur via stress reactions, which have a negative influence on children's physical health over time. Children could spend time thinking about the conflicts they are observing inside their family and analyzing the implications of such conflict-such as impending family breakdown or fear about abandonment-which can raise the overall stress that a youngster feels. Continual stress and self-blame may also lead to numerous other unwanted impacts on children, such as low-self esteem and self-worth, which eventually can impair a child's physical health and well-being. If youngsters are concerned and worried about home difficulties, they may also suffer from academic achievement because of their attention and incapacity to connect with meaningful social interactions.

One of the primary issues within this area of research is how precisely to define inter-parental conflict, given that some amount of conflict happens within all relationships and that conflict varied widely in its aggressiveness, intensity, and long-term occurrence. As such, researchers have generally focused on the frequency with which parents quarrel or participate in various conflict behaviors in purely numerical terms. Parental reports are typically utilized as well to establish how often and how severe conflict develops. These sorts of data gathering techniques are very frequently far from thorough, however, given that they do not take into consideration a broad range of elements that impacts how a youngster views the dispute in question. For instance, children have been observed to adapt better to conflict when the sort of conflict is one that they have seen repeatedly and feel more acquainted with.

Specific sorts of conflict have been related to particular types of behavioral disorders by certain meta-analyses' of the literature. For instance, the impact size for conflict that is stated openly is approximately double the amount of effect for conflict that is conveyed secretly. Overt conflict may be characterized as the conflict that is expressed in terms of hostile and aggressive behaviors, whereas covert conflict is conveyed indirectly. Such variations imply that parental handling of conflict might be more significant than when and how frequently conflict happens.

Impact sizes have not been associated with child gender or age, however, the amplitude of the effect was shown to be bigger for boys than for girls. Generally, data connecting the gender of the kid to the amount that they suffer developmental challenges linked with conflict have been inconsistent and have not led to any meaningful conclusions regarding the function of gender. Similarly, age is not a doctor of behavioral and or emotional difficulties in children as a consequence of inter-parental conflict, although it is understood that the initial years of a child's life are crucial for good emotional development. There are also extra issues connected to the ethnic compositions of children who make up study samples, with more research required in this area in the future.

Future Directions

The theory on inter-parental conflict and child development is only valuable since it can be converted into meaningful practice and participation. Even though countless efforts have been made to design programs that help parents, couples, and/or children, few of these programs have been exposed to rigorous or systematic reviews [6]. As well, the theoretical and empirical underpinning for programs that are designed frequently remains undetected or untested, so researchers are left to wonder whether programs are performing effectively and why. Cummings underlines the relevance of utilizing a transnational research methodology for the establishment and assessment of programs that expressly strive to transform research results into successful practice. Cumming created a curriculum based on Davies and Cummings Emotional Security Theory [EST] that applies a family-wide model for studying the impact of inter-parental conflict on children. Such programs that have a larger definition of inter-parental conflict and concentrate on the family more holistically have shown amazing potential for the future.

Conclusion

The inter-parental conflict has continuously been associated with bad results regard to respect for child development in terms of their physical, psychological, social, and emotional well-being. These negative effects occur via numerous methods that are both direct and indirect, including through the internalization of guilt and fear, and through the children's predisposition to replicate the behaviors they are observing routinely at home. Future programs that tackle these difficulties should concentrate on transferring research into practice so that such initiatives are anchored in strong theoretical and empirical research. More studies should also be aimed at identifying the boundaries and extent of inter-parental conflict, as well as concentrating on ethnic disparities in the connection between inter-parental conflict and child development. The subject of inter-parental conflict and children's emotional development is essential, particularly considering the enormous health and economic cost that this issue takes on governments and health care systems. In the future, this health concern should be a priority for politicians, practitioners, schools, and of course, parents.

Chapter 3

Effect of emotional parents

Problems between parents and children are widespread and timeless. If you are wanting to strengthen your connection with your parents, you are not alone. Developing a better connection with your parents entails examining the underlying source of the difficulties, establishing a more mature relationship with them, and concentrating on altering how you think and act. If you presently have a terrible connection with your parents, or a so-so relationship, but wish to improve it, several activities that may be done to make that happen.
Method 1\sChanging Yourself

✓ Stop Your Parents from Fighting
Act first. Don't wait for your parents to attempt to mend the connection. If you want to strengthen your connection with your parents, you should start right away and act first.
✓ Please Your Parents
Be grateful. Consider everything your parents have done for you; all the ways that they have benefited you; all the ways they have affected how you think. You may find yourself feeling thankful for your parents and more eager to mend the relationship or compromise or be more forgiving when your parents bother you.

Let your parents know that you are thankful for everything they have done for you. It may sting to be taken for granted, especially for parents.

Method 2\s Show your gratitude with your deeds.

Get them a lovely present or, if you live with your parents, do some additional cleaning without being asked. They will likely be delighted with you for this.

Method 3 \s Stop Your Parents from Fighting

Separate from your parents emotionally. This is not to argue that you should not care for and love your parents. But, if you are less emotionally tied to your parents, you may be less engaged in conflicts or disagreements with them. This way you may walk away from a situation more quickly and not let it destroy the relationship. You may remove yourself emotionally from your parents in two major ways.

Focus less on seeking their approval. Be willing to define yourself and your self-worth through your own eyes.

Acknowledge your history, then move forward. Your connection with your parents may have been poor earlier. Remember this and examine the part you have played in your relationship with your parents, but do not allow it to define your relationship moving ahead

Take their viewpoint. Often, individuals do not get along because they neglect to consider others' opinions. Once you can sympathize with another's stance and comprehend the reasoning behind it, you will likely be more inclined to compromise and enhance the connection.

Accept that your parents are different. They grew up at a different age with different social norms and standards of behavior, with different techniques and ways of thinking, with parents who treated them in particular ways, that were probably much different than the methods of parenting now. Think about the ways that their lives may have been different from your own, and how these diverse backgrounds may be contributing to troubles in the relationship.

Try utilizing this knowledge when you speak about strengthening your connection with them. Remind them that times change and invite them to reflect on their connection with their parents. See if they can recollect any challenges in their connection with their parents that were related to these 'generational' divides.

For example, if your relationship with your parents is rocky because they disapprove of you moving in with your significant other before marriage, try reminding them that in their generation people were even more conservative still and that times change and it is quite common to move in with a significant other without being married.

Method 4\s Change Your Life for the Better

Develop your own identity. It is OK and even good for you to think for yourself and to have your own opinion about topics. In developing a newfound feeling of autonomy and detachment from your parents, you may discover that your connection improves spontaneously.

Engage in self-discovery. Hold aside what everyone else believes about you and how you should conduct your life, especially your parents, and ask yourself some important questions about yourself. Be careful to honestly answer questions such as "what emotions do I want to feel most?" "what do I want to spend more of my time on?" or "what are my talents?" or "what sort of person am I?"

Consider if you are going along with your parents' perspective because you also believe it or because your innate tendency is to think about what they do about anything (such as regarding your relationships, politics, or even basic things like your favorite sports team, for example) (such as about your relationships, politics or even simple things like your favorite sports team, for example).

✓ Please Your Parents

Think of them as fellow grownups, not parents. If you continue to regard them as your parents, you may unthinkingly act in a manner that is child-like and fosters a relationship dynamic that you are attempting to repair.

For example, if you continue to expect them to assist you financially, you may be keeping the door open for your parents to offer you too much unwelcome advice or shame you into spending time with them.

1

Figure out the fundamental reason. Assess what in particular is upsetting you about your connection with your parents. There are various reasons you may desire to better your relationship.

You may feel that your parents offer too much-unwanted advice, treat you like a child, do not respect your thoughts, shame you into spending time with them, or disdain your friends or spouse. Be sure to have a solid grasp of the specific component of your relationship that you want to change.

2\s Be respectful. Even if you do not agree with their parenting style, morals or ideas, remain respectful to your parents; in doing so you will be less likely to throw them into a defensive parenting posture.

There are a lot of ways in which you may be courteous. Try using polite language (such as "sorry" or "would you mind if"), speaking modestly ("it may be" instead of "it certainly is"), and letting them complete speaking before you have your turn.

3

Don't let things fester. If you quarrel with your parents, do all you can to mend the connection sooner rather than later. This will convey that you care about the connection. It will also mean you will have been battling for less time in total

4

Keep calm. Don’t overreact while talking to your parents, you may wind up saying things you regret, which will only hurt your relationship more and make you appear immature.

When you are dealing with your parents and you sense a wave of high emotion coming on, re-assess the circumstances that led to your strong sentiments by asking yourself these questions.

For example, if you are in a debate with your parents over mowing the lawn you can ask: "In the broad scheme of things, how horrible would it be to mow the grass?"

Or, if you don't live with your parents but they are unduly engaged, asking you specific questions about your career and providing unwelcome advice, you may ask: "What is their purpose for wanting to be so involved? Is it that they care about me and are anxious about my financial security?" Asking yourself questions like these may cause you to feel less unhappy and it may provide you insight into how you should react to your parents. In this scenario, you may attempt to strengthen your connection by soothing their anxieties about your financial future.

If re-assessing your circumstance doesn't help to minimize how emotional you feel, consider asking respectfully if you can resume the talk after you have cooled your jets. Explain that you are feeling particularly sad and don’t want to mistakenly say anything harsh or regretful.

5

Be positive. Smile at your parents. Stay cheerful and warm. Let them know via your body language that you are delighted to see them and that you care about their well-being. This will establish the tone for your discussion and will assist to enhance the connection. Without realizing it, your parents may even replicate your pleasant sentiments. This emotional mimicking will assist in generating an atmosphere that will support good relationship improvement.

6

Don't seek their counsel unless you genuinely want it. Sometimes issues occur in relationships between parents and children, especially during the teenage years and beyond, since parents might attempt to provide counsel in an overbearing manner that infringes on your feeling of autonomy.

To get around this, consider only asking for their advice when you are sure that you want it. If you are simply feeling lazy to think about things on your own, and so you ask your parents, you may be opening the door to irritation on your side.

7

Be frank. One strategy to enhance your relationship dynamic is to be more open to speaking to your parents about topics that you may feel are unpleasant. This will assist to create trust in your connection with your parents, which will strengthen your relationship with them.

Keep in frequent communication so your parents may gain a better perspective on your life, what concerns you, and what makes you happy. If they do not know you very well, it will be tough for them to strive to strengthen the connection. If you listen to your parents they will be more inclined to listen to you, opening the door for you to attempt to discuss repairing the connection.

8

Establish limits and create regulations. If you want to keep a great connection with your parents, but find that you usually wind up arguing, try putting up specific subjects as off-limits. This may work better if you are older or no longer live with your parents. Also, consider making rules that both you and your parents agree to adhere to.

Sit down with your parents and explain to them you want to better your connection with them, but that to do so, you believe it would be good if there were some regulations. Ask that they produce a list of the regulations they would want to be enacted, and you do the same.

If you are a teenager or kid, guidelines might include avoiding bringing up particular issues, allowing you a chance to try things on your own, or letting you remain out later at night as long as you check in by text or phone and can establish that you are being responsible.

If you are an adult, guidelines might include asking your parents not to interfere with the way you are choosing to raise your children, or asking your parents not to talk harshly about your significant other.

Discuss the various rules, then reduce them down to a list that you all agree on. Check you and your parents are still satisfied with obeying the regulations that you have agreed to.

9\s Avoid needless arguments. Sometimes fights are inevitable but try your best to prevent needless squabbles. This may imply that you have to bite your tongue when one of your parents says something contentious. Determine if the urge to react is genuinely required. If it is, make the point clearly and modestly to avoid an overly emotional argument.

10

Keep interactions mature. Be fair and logical about issues and demonstrate to your parents that you are mature, and they will likely reciprocate by acting maturely. Oftentimes if parents perceive you behaving adult, they will treat you similarly.

Chapter 4

Types of emotional parents

What it takes to have a cordial relationship with emotional parents

The 4 categories of emotionally immature parents

They are stiff and single-minded and may get extremely defensive when individuals have opposing beliefs.

They have low-stress tolerance and have problems acknowledging errors, rejecting the facts, and blaming others instead.

They do what feels best, typically following the route of least resistance.

They show little regard for other people's varied beliefs and opinions.

They are self-preoccupied and egotistical.

They have minimal empathy and are emotionally insensitive.

They dread sensations and could have taught their children that some feelings are shameful or “bad”.

They concentrate attention on the physical instead of emotional requirements of their children.

They may be killjoys, reacting to their children’s ideas or excitement dismissively or doubtfully.

They have powerful yet superficial emotions and are often fast to respond.

As an adult, you may now experience:

Lingering sentiments of wrath, loneliness, betrayal, or abandonment.

Feeling guilty about being miserable.

Feeling exceedingly sensitive and receptive to other pcople.

Difficulty trusting your instincts.

Lacking self-confidence.

Feeling imprisoned in taking care of your parent(s) (s).

People with emotionally immature parents typically feel emotionally lonely around their parents, even while they’re together. While there is often a large emphasis on the physical demands that were addressed, there is little to no attention on the emotional needs.

This may be problematic for kids who grew up with a parent like this since they are inclined to dismiss their issues in the future. They could assume that they shouldn't have anything to complain about since their experience wasn't "bad enough" compared to others who did not have their bodily needs addressed.

Being a parent is much more than simply giving clothes, a house over your head, and food on the table. For children to develop into healthy adults, they need to feel secure and encouraged to grow, be recognized, and express themselves.

Most emotionally immature parents have little knowledge of how they've harmed their children. To be clear, we aren't casting blame on these parents, we are looking to understand why they are the way they are. The purpose here is to assist you to get fresh insights into your parent(s) to develop your self-awareness and emotional independence.

Keep in mind that each kind occurs along a range, from moderate to severe, with varying degrees of narcissism.

Emotional parents

The emotionally immature parent is generally governed by their emotions. They respond to tiny disruptions like the end of the world and tend to depend on external stimuli, such as other people or intoxicants to calm and stabilize them. The emotional parent will likely swing from being too active in their child's life to sudden retreat. These parents are prone to instability and unpredictability and have been termed, by Dr. Lindsay Gibson, as the most infantile of the four categories of emotionally immature parents.

Driven parents

The motivated parent tends to seem the most normal out of the four kinds, even looking very involved in their children's life. However, these parents are very controlling and meddling, seldom stopping long enough to develop meaningful empathy and emotional connection with their children. Instead, the motivated parent is generally busy and excessively goal-oriented. They generally expect everyone to desire and appreciate the same things they do.

Passive parents

The passive parent often avoids dealing with anything uncomfortable. They are frequently the "favorite" parent, looking more emotionally accessible than the other kinds, but only up to a certain point. The passive parent seldom provides their children with any meaningful limitations or instruction to assist them to navigate the world. They enjoy taking a backseat to a domineering spouse, even allowing abuse and neglect to occur by looking the other way. The passive parent copes by minimizing issues and acquiescing.

Rejecting parents

The rejected parent generally wants to be left alone. They typically govern the family and house, everything revolves around them, and the family automatically attempts to not offend them. These parents exhibit little to no intimacy or actual contact with their children, and their interactions consist of delivering directives, blowing up, or distancing themselves from family life. When confronted with efforts to bring them into loving or emotional exchanges, the rejecting parent will typically withdraw oneself.

How to avoid being absorbed in emotional parents

I sensed her sorrow and loneliness as if they were my own. Even as I type that line, my eyes flood up and sorrow fills my heart. Then, I'm reminded to implement the advice I offer others.

My mom was a wonderful person, a sensitive soul much like myself. I'm so much like she was, but so different. One of the contrasts between us is that I had a chance to watch her life's problems. I saw her struggles mirrored inside myself and made a deliberate decision to discover healthy methods to deal with them.

You see, my mom was a profound feeler and sensed the emotions of people near and distant. I suppose it was her tremendous empathy and personal problems that caused her to desire to assist others, as a wounded healer in a manner.

But as a helper and healer, she suffered with her mental and emotional health throughout the years. Witnessing her life inspired me to learn how to moderate my own sensitive emotions and create appropriate limits.

Sometimes I wonder if not understanding how to handle her empathy is what got her ill.

There are numerous ways to comprehend the problems my mum endured until she died in 2007. From her viewpoint, she had an unusual, undiscovered medical disease. Some who knew her may have believed she was manipulative and attention-seeking. Some might perceive an addiction to pain drugs. Psychologists would diagnose her with the psychosomatic condition, borderline personality disorder, and bipolar disorder.

Maybe all and none of those explanations are accurate. But possibly she didn't have any "disorder" at all. I'm not declaring anything to be true, but rather offering an intriguing question. What if she was merely a sensitive, empathetic person who could not handle the grief around and inside her? What if one ineffective coping method led to a whole ll of other ailments?

I think my mum endured true physical and mental suffering. I tried to completely comprehend her throughout the years. But after many years of thought, I now believe in her expertise because of what I know about my sensitive nature.

As sensitive persons, we may present with strong emotions and feel easily overwhelmed by our senses. We're frequently informed by the world that there's something wrong with us. And when we believe there's something essentially wrong with ourselves, we tend to put these tendencies away into our "shadow" or unconscious mind.

Well, now we've not only tucked away our inner nature but maybe the empathetic depth that goes along with being a sensitive person as well. There may be a part of us that recognizes that we're emotional sponges. Yet, we may choose to reject our nature without actually learning how to control our empathy in such a manner that avoids "dis-ease" and supports well-being.

This was me for a long time.

Not only am I prone to feeling tired and drained in settings with particular individuals, but the emotional suffering of others tends to show itself in my physical body. When I over-feel, my throat feels like it's shutting and when my chest constricts, my persistent back pain flares up.

My lover was complaining of one of those little, uncomfortable pimples inside his nose lately. I received one as well. We joked about sympathy aches, but I do wonder occasionally. I've felt the emotional suffering of my family, friends, clients, and strangers. It's not a simple, "Oh, I feel horrible for him." It's experiencing the sadness and rejection of the youngster whose parents didn't pick him up when he was discharged from the psychiatric hospital where I worked. It's the profound sorrow of being that relative who thinks no one believes her and she's all alone.

I am challenged to find the perfect vocabulary to explain it all since the profound pain and heavy load is a feeling not a term.

The point is that no matter how difficult it is to feel the weight of the world in my body, I wouldn't give my depth and capacity to feel for anything. The empathy that comes with heightened sensitivity is a real gift if we know how to utilize it.

We need more gentle, sensitive hearts if we wish to repair the planet. Sensitive individuals have a natural propensity to exhibit compassion because of our tremendous sensitivity.

Deep empathy offers us a distinct power in interacting and connecting to others. When we sincerely care, we're more inclined to be able to grasp another person in a manner not that all individuals can. Our genuineness may assist us to build meaningful, rewarding connections.

Relationships allow us a chance to not only build a profound feeling of connection with another human being, but also an opportunity to learn about ourselves. Both of these are important to the human experience.

And as sensitive beings, we not only sense the severity of suffering, but also the intensity of delight.

Yet, managing our empathy is crucial to avoiding the torrent of feeling from overpowering our capacity to manage and care for our well-being.

If we wish to quit absorbing emotional baggage from others, it all begins with taking care of our bodily, social, mental, emotional, and spiritual needs. I know it seems like the entire world is harping on the notion of self-care, but there's a purpose for this.

When our own immune system or vitality is exhausted, we become a great sponge for sopping up emotions. We must take care of ourselves to prevent absorption in the first place.

1. When you observe intense emotion, start by identifying what you're experiencing.
Labeling serves to put us into a condition of pause, which might assist us to gain a little distance from the emotional experience for a minute.

2. Ask yourself if what you're experiencing is yours, someone else's, or a combination of the two.
It might be tough to distinguish the difference occasionally. One way I prefer to use is if I believe I may

be experiencing a certain individual's "stuff," I'll image the person as entirely whole, happy, and full of light. Then I'll reexamine my own experience and see whether I still feel the same way.

This played out in a recent loss in my life. While I was suffering my loss, when my relative who was closest to this person started to start to heal, I discovered that much of my sadness dissipated as well.

3. The instant you notice yourself experiencing emotions that aren't yours, heighten your awareness of what's occurring inside you.
It might help to speak the word "compassion" to yourself as a means of actively concentrating on what you can do to be helpful rather than allowing yourself to be overtaken by emotion.

4. Take a deep breath and identify where in your body you feel the most peaceful, grounded, or neutral.
It may be as basic as your toe or finger. Bring your attention to that location in your body and allow it to be a centering force to keep you grounded as you process and release whatever emotions you may have collected. Sometimes simply having one quiet region in our body might act as a resource when the rest of you is feeling stressed.

5. Return the other person's feelings to them.
It is not your obligation to bear other people's emotional suffering, and as essential, it helps absolutely no one.

Try repeating to yourself, “I’m letting this emotional suffering that is not mine go now.” Remember that other individuals have to go through their processes to evolve.

6. Use visualization to entirely release the feelings.
I find that it helps me to envision a waterfall running through my body as the last discharge of whatever lingering emotional garbage I may be harboring.

—

At the crux of all of the aforementioned processes is growing the awareness to realize when we’re allowing ourselves to absorb and adopting measures to lessen this predisposition. As a sensitive person, your empathy is a gift that the world needs. It’s up to each of us to turn our empathy into deeper compassion so that we can stay healthy and well.

Chapter 5

Ways to deal with emotional parents

[1] Dealing with Your Parents

✓Manage the problem.

If your parents are being extremely emotional or anxious, it is typically simpler to control the situation instead of participating in it. If you need to acquire anything particular from them or speak to them about something specific, try to be straightforward with your queries or within your conversation. If you avoid reacting emotionally, your parents may be more inclined to respond in a similar method. Even if they don't, you will be less likely to get stressed from the contact if you only seek to control them instead of joining in their emotional, anxious behavior.

For example, if your parents are raising their voices at you, don't raise yours back. Calmly attempt to continue the talk without making things worse.

✓help the problem.

If you notice what is creating the stress or emotional behavior in your parent's life, attempt to assist with it if you can. There may be certain instances where you can't assist, such as personal concerns with their relationship or their interactions with others, or in some cases money troubles, but there are other situations where you can aid. Even releasing just a bit of the pressure will assist deescalate the situation to where your parents may calm down.

For example, if you realize that an untidy home is causing your parents to stress out, consider tidying up around the house or washing the dishes. Or if you are old enough to have a job, get a job and start purchasing some of your goods or give your parents a small bit of money to assist with things.

✓Talk to them about it.

If your parents are too worried and emotional for you to cope with, speak to them about it. Have real instances of how they have behaved that have stressed you out or been overly emotional. Don't criticize or accuse them of awful conduct, simply explain to them that they have been unusually emotional and anxious recently and that it is interfering with your life. Most parents may not even realize how they have been behaving or know how it is hurting them.

Make sure you do this gently. Even if your parents fight back with harsh words or can't see what they've been doing, make sure you keep calm. You can only do so much in these circumstances. Once you've informed them, it is up to them to modify it. If it still doesn't alter over time, try having the topic again with new instances of their conduct.

[2] Listening to the Parents

✓Make thoughtful remarks.
Sometimes when parents are extremely emotional, it may be difficult for them to remain focused. Use phrases like that starting with something like, "What I am hearing you say is," or, "I can sense from your voice how emotional you are." These remarks will let them know you recognize their emotions
You may also utilize affirming remarks such as, "That must be incredibly tough" to let the parents realize you are listening and taking their stress, feelings, and worries seriously.

[3] Encouraging Self Care.

✓Suggest self-care for the parent's stress. As anybody will tell you, parenting is the hardest job you can have. Sometimes, when parents are over-emotional, it might be useful if you advise them to take some time and space to care for themselves. By doing this, you are again demonstrating support, indicating that you are listenlng, and helping reduce their tension by permitting them to concentrate on themselves
Depending on the severity of the circumstance, you may need to advise various things. For example, if there has been a loss in the family, urge the parent to seek therapy. Offer to link them with free services, or advise the parent to contact their insurance company to locate

a therapist that can assist them. The parent may be beyond their power to properly manage what is going on in their family, and seeking the support of a professional may be the best thing for them and their kid.

✓Ask the parents what they need.

It could assist you to ask the parents what they believe they may need to get through their stressed feelings. See if there is anything you can do to assist, such as proposing parenting courses or books. Depending on what is troubling the youngster, maybe a support group might be useful and you can assist them to discover one.

For example, if the parents have an autistic kid and are strained beyond their limitations, a support group for parents with autistic children may be a terrific method for them to reduce feelings of loneliness and connect with other parents with similar concerns.

✓Emphasize the necessity for emotional stability.

Impress upon the parents how vital their emotional condition is for the well-being of not only themselves but also their kids. Sometimes parents might forget themselves in the everyday pressures of job and child care, and it can be good to hear that their mental wellness is vital and legitimate. Tell the parent that they matter, their emotions count, and even if you care for their kid as your profession, part of caring for that child is caring for the whole family.

Be a pillar of support and affirmation for stressed parents. In the long term, improved emotional health in the parents provides for better emotional health for the kid. As a youth worker, your goal is to promote arenas for healthy children. Be gentle, listen, affirm, and sympathize when parents are worried.

Chapter 6

Recognizing emotional parents

Below we have collected tell-tale indicator you have a emotional parents.

1.Rigid and Single-Minded
Is your parents a "my way or the highway" sort of person? sort of person? Do they feel defensive if someone recommends an alternate method of completing or thinking about something?

Is it hard for hard to grasp when desires something different from them?

These are features of emotional parents

1. Low-Stress Tolerance
   Many emotionally childish parents have a low stress tolerance. They cannot deal when things go wrong and have difficulties acknowledging errors and flaws.

   Individuals that display this habits overlook facts and cling to myths they have formed in their heads. They also incline to blame others.

2. Low-Conflict Tolerance

   In addition to low-tress tolerance, emotionally adolescent have a low-conflict tolerance. They prefer to push problems under the proverbial rug rather than dealing with them head-on. When you want to clear the air about a problem, they refuse and attempt to gaslight you for being over pushy or needy. Moreover, they are prone to what feels best for them instead of emphasizing the broader good.

3. Emotionally Ignorant

   Low emotionally IQs are are empathy level are frequent among emotionally incompetent persons. For them, everything is black and white, and they have problems connecting that hasn't directly impacted them.

   They may offer a lot of lip service when something horrible occurs, but it's typically not sincere.

   Emotionally illiterate individuals frequently shun counseling and say it's "Junk of silence" that won't improve anything. But they're scared of someone seeing the true them...seeing the true them.

www.ingramcontent.com/pod-product-compliance
Lightning Source LLC
LaVergne TN
LVHW052107160826
845678LV00015B/3402
9798846631014